Don Wa

In the Shed

To Philip and Margaret

Thanks for your friendship.

Love,
Don

First published in 2005 by
DEADGOOD Publications
England

Copyright © Don Walls 2005

Cover illustration by Don Walls
Typeset by Emily Harker
Printed by Abbey Print, North Yorkshire, England

For my friends

CONTENTS

Relationships	1
Tortoise	2
Fibs	3
The Lament of the Door Knob	4
Doodling	5
Carpets	6
Positive Thinking	7
Weeding	8
Tea in the Garden	9
I woke up one morning	10
Bookmite	11
Pet Number	12
Triangle	13
Norm	14
Love Story	15
Myself	16
Armadillo	17
For Mary	18
Retirement	19
When I Retire	20
For A	21
Keeping a Wasp	22
The Carpenter	23
Mary told me *this* herself	24
Cows	25
Mr Wake	26
Driving	27
Pigs	28
Joke	29
Circle Fancier	30
My Bottom	31
States of Mind	32
Hands	33
Album	34
For Banjo	35

CONTENTS (continued)

There were murmurs down the lane	36
Starlings	37
The day after the blitz	38
Chocolate Cake, Fishing and the Germans	39
Upstream	40
I was four or five	41
For my Mother	42
Heron	43
On Going Back	44
It was the light that kept me	45
Second Thoughts	46
Horse	47
My Pet Hate	48
Manic Depression	49
Before (i)	50
On the Southern Side of the Taurus	51
Hattusha	52
For Ainslee	53
Everyday we went down to the beach	54
Geranium	55
In the Shed	56
Poem for Christmas	57
there was a woman	58
They've planted plastic roses	59
Early morning and I sit at the window	60
I am a keeper of the letter z's	61
Once upon a time there was a number	62
Starling	63
Before (ii)	64
Us Fingers	65
That day by the sea	66
Balding	67
disorientation	68
Shoes	69
Before (iii)	70

Relationships

I have lived with lines all my life,
most prop each other up - triangles, squares.
Some do their own thing - zigzag, squiggle
and some like circles are self-contained,
but the lines that are closest are parallel lines
intuitively knowing where each is going
whether straight or curved - performing duets,
sometimes looping the world together.
Horizons away, they seem to converge
but in reality, never touch,
yet parallel lines never go their own way
the space between them keeps them together.

Tortoise

I walked with him round the yard.
He dawdled and I was late for school.
I polished the patterns on his shell
and stroked his head,
enticed him with a lettuce leaf.
No teeth, he cut out pieces with his sharp-edged mouth.
I sprinkled him with water in the sun,
and sometimes in a box, I carried him to the Ings.
He explored the grasses.
I wondered what wildness meant to him.
I filed his nails.
Autumn and I brought him in
and he slept the Winter in the cupboard,
tapping on the door in Spring,
eager for greenness, light.

That September I left him in the yard all night
and Winter came early,
'tortoise tortoise' rang in my head.
The frost glistened on his shell.
I stared and shivered.

Fibs (For John and Kay)

I foster fibs.
They reside in the shed.
My wife won't have them in the house.

I run courses for them on camouflage and melting into speech,
the meeting of eyes and innocence.

My fibs are dependable, brave sometimes
standing their ground in the face of fact.
Between me and my fibs, there's trust, respect.
A discarded fib has nowhere to go.
To survive, some fibs weave fibs round fibs
- these fibs are never honest fibs.
A fib must be true to itself.

Once at a congress of nationwide fibbers
last in a line of eminent speakers
- churchmen, lawyers -
I presented my fib.
Oh the hurrahs, the standing ovation!

Fibs breed, of course, and there are various species:
greater fibs and lesser fibs,
numerous as the birds round my garden shed.
And sometimes there are transmutations:
bloated lies.
Of these I get rid lest they affect the bona fide fibs.
Most fibs are gentle, harmless.
Everyday they feed from my hand.

The Lament of the Door Knob

We're mainly unnoticed
except for crystal, brass polished bright
porcelain sometimes,
but most of us are bakelite
and spend a lifetime in service.

No burden too great,
they hang anything on us
- bags of bottles, a brace of pheasants.
Kids swing on us, the strain
sometimes gets us down.
(Our name, of course, they take in vain).
They wrench and twist us
clench a fist and batter the door
sending a tremor through our spindles.
We wobble with age.

I often wonder what would happen
if we all disappeared at 7 a.m.,
half the nation would be locked in the loo
- imagine the mayhem
or at the passage of bills, laws
would depend on the opening of doors.

In fact, everything works when everything works,
it's all down to function, not status
yet that's how they rate us.

Doodling

I was addicted to doodling early on,
it ran in the family.
My Grandfather doodled through the First World War
- decorative doodling round Grandmother's letters
and my father doodled hyperbolas, ellipses,
like lines he cast on the River Wharfe.
We were a dynasty of doodlers.
My mother said I doodled in the womb.

Vowels I transformed with hats and eyes, legs of octopodes.
Pages of Kandinsky art.
My first report 'Would do better if he doodled less'.
I sang in the choir
- the prayer book a Godsend through acres of sermons.
'The devil's distraction,' the vicar said.
Inspired by Thompson's mouse,
I doodled on pews.

Then, I doodled on sex,
navy blue stockings and snowy thighs
that flashed upon that inward eye in English, French.
Once I was caught doodling tits and bums
round Shakespeare's sonnets. They told my mum.
'And has no appreciation of the Art of the Bard'.
(I thought of Falstaff, the tart Doll Tearsheet).
My parents embarrassed. My peers impressed.

And doodling spread:
each night in my head Bardot my paramour
- Jane Russel, Jean Simmons…
I could doodle on anything - politics, religion,
but nowadays mostly I doodle on words and make a poem.
It all began with a squiggle.
Last week in the library I watched a beginner,
his hesitant pencil skittering the pages.
Oh, I could have shown him how to do it!

Carpets

They think we're nobodies
spineless, shat upon

made love upon
pissed upon

crucified from wall to wall.

We're all depressed,
kneaded by cats and seared by ash.

(The ceiling, the bastard, serene looks down).

A slip of a mat sidles away,

everyday they fetch her back.
The dogs have chewed her fringes off.

The door mat's choking in dusty rage.

Everyone walks over us, our posture prostrate
in dreams and prayers, our vision
pubic.

We know humanity from bottom to top.

Positive Thinking

Metal urinals turn me on,
I love the skill of bingo
and played, of course, fortissimo
The Top of the Pops.

I've bought a mobile phone
make calls in pubs, Next and Gap,
the Royal Albert Hall.
It sharpens, of course, my driving skills.

I wear designer clothes
and things are wicked, cool or crap.
I club all night,
drink only from the bottle neck
wear t-shirts in the mist and cold.
This I find attracts the chicks,

and positive par excellence
Ruby Thatcher turns me on
and so does Margaret Wax

Weeding. Every year, weeding early Spring.
With no resistance - some by the roots.
Tufted, break off,
the ground elder determined to stay.

I sift the leaves - toadstools, woodlice
and the black earth, ages of it,
ingrained in my palms, under my nails.
I'm surprised at shoots I'd forgotten were there.

A crocus in the greyness. A robin.
The same one perhaps in the wake of my weeding a year ago,

and at the garden's end the goose grass clings.
I tear it from my clothes
and crouch by the tree my Father cut down.
I touch the rings - the years somehow.

Tea in the Garden

We had tea in the garden
- all proper set out, sandwiches, cakes.
My Father, Mother and I in an old-fashioned Summer.
No rain for weeks. Weeds dying,
and my Mother in the shade in her rocking chair
and my Father praising the blooms he'd watered everyday
when over the rooftops clouds
- the mist of rain,
then huge spots darkening, a drumming on the shed,
and runnels not knowing where to flow,
the dust of Summer on their backs
- trees, roses, delphinia drenched,
the soil gulping.
My Father drenched, my Mother drenched
just standing there facing the rain.
Wild, I pulled my shirt off.

I woke up one morning
and whatever I touched turned to chocolate
- pins and things
fireguard, kettle
teapot glugging
clotted zip and gooey buttons
and a razor as blunt as a chocolate truffle.

Philanthropist, in the shadows
I baited muggers
then froze them hard in chocolate death
and smashed them up in waste for kids.
I am the children's chocolate saviour
- they follow me across the Ings and round the block
licking gateposts, chocolate privet
sheds, soft and wobbly in the melting sun.

I can chocolatise anything, anywhere,
but wear chocolate proof gloves
to stroke my dog
and for making love.

Gloveless once I touched a Prime Minister.
Stricken in chocolate,
the crowd immediately gobbled him up.

Bookmite

In the mirror of his eyes I glimpse myself
- my white safari across the page, his nose a promontory,
valleys of despair running up from the mouth,
his face the steppes of Central Asia, everywhere scrub.
Calm sometimes, then the hot sirocco
and you never know what weathering next
with miles to go across the whiteness
- his world a mystery,
shifting expressions like sand in the wind
- first a smile and then a smirk, a muscle away,
a questioning - something in the open spaces,
the sorrow of emptiness under the stars,
and what he thinks I never know.
I stop sometimes in the warmth of his eyes
and then the threat
and I run for cover in the film of air between the pages.

Pet Number

I keep a pet number inside my shed
and watch him transform himself by self calculation,

squaring, cubing himself
increasing himself by the power 'n',

though he never shows off, just practises skills.

Once he could have become the largest number in the Universe
ribbons of noughts floating through space,
but then he faced the other way
and calculating a minus dimension existed on the other side.

Imagine existing on the other side!

A metaphysical pet number inside your shed
with the potential to multiply or vanish even.

They are unusual pets.

Of course, they will not fetch a stick.
They do not sit on your lap nor feed from your hand,
but with numbers you know where you are
- clean as picked bones - all intellect.

They neither love nor hate.

I keep a triangle in the garden shed and walk him everyday.
He's well-bred
and like all triangles adores circles.
Yesterday he saw one on the Ings
and before you could say parallelogram
he put his head straight through her.
Incensed, her mistress said:
'Pedigree, now pregnant'.
The triangle hid behind my legs.
The simpering circle was dragged away.

Some weeks later, I walked my triangle on the Ings
and we saw the circle
and romping behind her six little cuddly things
- circular triangles or triangular circles.
(My triangle, of course, was filled with pride.)
I'd like to keep one in the garden shed.

Norm

And in walked the Norm
a pair of shears in his hand.
He reduced the hedge to standard height
and the lawn to bald nothingness.
He clipped my hair
and without a passport entered my head
and cut down thoughts.
Others he trimmed.
Some Norms take up residence in your head for years on end.
Eviction orders don't apply.
If you drive them out, overnight they're back again.
Eventually they die of natural causes,
but another appears
- that's the way it is with Norms
when one expires another takes over.
Their brief - to rummage your head for aberrant growth.

Once in my head two Norms appeared, each with shears.
Norms, of course, are singular creatures who hate each other.
They clashed and clipped each other to death.

For one glorious day
I walked in my head in the silence of the Yorkshire Wolds.
It was a Normless, sunlit day.

Love Story

Once upon a time there was a full stop
who fell in love with a comma.

He followed her the full length of the page.
When she paused, he stopped.

At night he slipped along the pure-white lane.
She came out to meet him.

Sometimes they danced, their heads so close
it seemed a comma danced on her own.

Together they romped in the snow-white margin.

Imagine! The snow-white margin
and love beyond words.

Myself

Trousers crumpled on the bedroom floor,
my habits follow me at heel like dogs
bark my presence to myself.
Toothpaste clogs my brush
- I am an obstacle to myself.

So when Jim's away I move next door,
pretend that I am someone else,
but they follow me there:
my socks on the floor, my shape in the bed,
wherever I am, I'm always there.

Armadillo (For Mary and Me)

In the park that day Mary led me to the monkey tree
where, on the earth beneath, a bald hedgehog unfurled
and feeling clever *erinaceus europaeus*, I classified the beast.
Mary eyed me from top to toe and then unleashed a word in Greek
'*Dasypodidae*, Armadillo,' she said.
'Well it must have escaped from a zoo,' I thought.
'No,' she said, endowed with the gift of reading my thoughts
'Like the big Black Cats of Bodmin Moor
it's always been here - it goes back to Pangea'.
I feigned knowledge and nodded.
Then from her patent leather bag she drew a leash,
crimson with a golden collar
and slipped it round the dillo's neck
and polished his bones with a shammy leather.
She sprinkled the beast with Eau de Cologne
and placed a rose behind his ear.
Then they lolloped ahead. I jogged behind.
He mounted her leg.
'Playful,' she said and patted his head.
I dared the thought of his true intent
and Mary swung round with a look of contempt.
'Typical Scorpio,' she said
and mimicking Mary the beast narrowed his eyes
eyeing me down the full length of his snout.
Then he leapt ahead and licked her hand and I said to myself
'a fawning, porcine, noxious slaverer'
and Mary spun round thunderous black.
Then they lolloped round the park again
and with night seeping in along the borders through the trees
she made his bed with crispy leaves
and settled him down and stroked his snout.
He eyed me smugly.
Then we left the park Mary and I
and I said to myself, 'I'll ring the RSPCA
and they'll take the armoured pig away.'
'They won't,' she said and patted my head
and coiled a leash around my neck
and tweaked my nose.
Behind my ear she placed a rose.
She showered my hair with Eau de Cologne.
We lolloped home.

For Mary

Smiles - caught in memory as they touched your face,
these are rare:
on your lips in sleep
or glimpsed through tears.

These - notes upon their habitat:
the North York Moors in the purple time,
beating the tide at Lindisfarne,
and this one special
- we searched above Kilburn for the White Horse
in snow.

Retirement

At first I tried to organise it,
but it has a mind of its own
- gets up late,
takes a nap in the afternoon,
perky by evening with a good red wine.
It drifts through the day coming in late.
The neighbours have noticed it.
I think they're envious.
Most of all, it likes to watch people going to work.
Sometimes it just sits and watches me paint.

When I Retire

When I retire
I'll keep giraffes in the garden
    mottle the house
    yellow and brown.

Late at night they'll move me on
    and I'll encourage weeds,
    and words kept in the bottom drawer
from adolescence,

and learn from children
because their logic's lovely.
    My intellect - groomed for years -
    I'll let run wild

and go on safari when I like
since all that's rare is

sudden in the long grass.

For A

I open your book at petals pressed in the bloom of time:

this buttercup,
now faintly yellow
veils random clusters of little words,

recalling somehow that Summer's chatter
of harebells and dreams

- this grass you picked,
this forget-me-not
that keeps its colour.

Keeping a Wasp

In the jar his world is round
and the only sound
the buzz of himself
and no way out
- frantic for footholds
frazzled hums, hunched,

so boost his esteem,
praise his stripes
- tiger among insects,
his valour
- flailed away, zig zag attacks,

needs to dream
so tell him stories of Shangri-la:
everything ambrosial
honey trees, nectar
- a buzz of euphoria
brimming the jar,

and squash him a kiss,
lips on the glass.
He longs to be noticed,
indifference destroys
even hate resuscitates,
so take the lid off
shout 'shite'
- a little aggression, he will buzz into life.

The Carpenter (For my Father)

As if some quiet communion held
between himself and the wood he shaped,
he knew where to cut and where to plane,
what joint to make;
fingers following the living grain,
everything dovetailed in his hands -
that stool, that clothes-rack
over there,
this table, this chair
where I feel his palm
rest gently on my back.

Mary told me *this* herself:

there was a man who used his giraffe
for cleaning windows round the town:

the bucket held in the animal's mouth,
the man shinned up the dappled neck.

Behind its ear it wore a rose,
from window boxes nibbled flowers.

Seeing a giraffe in panes of glass,
it lathered and licked the windows clean.

Great with kids, they chuted down its dappled neck.

It arched to let the traffic pass
and left its presence everywhere:
the Lord Mayor's steps, outside Next
Liberty's, Browns,

so the Council met and the beast was banished
to Whipsnade Zoo.

Losing its lofty self-esteem, it wouldn't eat
and bowed its neck.
It died depressed.

As for the man,
his ladder dappled yellow, brown,
a red rose bloomed behind his ear.

And Mary told me *this* herself:
he nibbled herbs from her window-box.

Cows

Over the hedge steam curling,
odour of fresh cowpats.
Herefords (their blankets of colour - white, brick red)
hurried down to meet me, udders swinging
heavy with milk,
in a curious circle surrounded me
and one came close her breath on my hand,
then bellowed from her belly's depth
and she was not just saying hello to kindred cows fields away.

The rooks flapped off.
In the half-light a fox slipped through the hedge.

She stared at me
wondering who I was beneath the high beech and lime.
I stood there into the soft night
- the stars, the moon rising
and glimpsed myself in her dark wild eyes.

Mr Wake

Trim, navy suit,
boots coal bright
Victorian moustache
benevolent, retired
Grandad-man
- Mr.Wake
always had time for time of day
his gossip rich
his gospel word
the back lane truth on wars, weather
- his addiction, horses.
The 'Sporting Pink' he read aloud,
scribbling his bets on a packet of fags.
'Any luck today?' neighbours asked
'Tanner on Danny Boy,
got pipped at the post,
but Dante's a cert at Newmarket for the three o'clock.'
And when he won
oh when he won!
generous as orchards to us kids
slipped lollies, laughed
and threepenny bits.

After the Ebor, 1942,
all betting stopped.
The wind blew flinty down the lane
us kids in groups
some shadow sun
a Woodbine packet lay on the ground
faded, wet
you could just make out an odds on favourite
for the five o'clock.

Driving

I like driving on my own and talking to myself.
It's good to talk to someone who never contradicts
- views identical, language.
No-one else in the car you can shout or whisper
do it all in your head
and even before he opens his mouth you know what he'll say.

Looking back I glimpse him in my driving mirror,
darkness on the road behind
- the miles we've travelled blank
and driving on, the moon
we can't catch up with down a country road.

Late at night we stop sometimes
and wonder where we are.
We share the same silence.

Pigs

They bask in the warmth of straw
and you wouldn't know they were there
if their sighs didn't sometimes
let them down like tyres,
or their legs twitch in pig dreams.

Rattle a bucket and they emerge
with squeals of appetite
for swill. Pushing and chopping
they guzzle anything - tails
twirling in lust for food.

They're great for kids
rooting in muck and flopping down
like the Great White sow,
I've always preferred them
to sheep or cows.
They grunt. They're bare.

Joke

I have a favourite joke.
My wife is tired of it so I keep it in the shed
and groom it everyday.
I roll around in stitches.

Once past midnight friends dropped in to hear my joke,
their laughter boisterous buffeting the sides of the garden shed,
and the police arrived.
'And what's the joke?' they said.
I told them,
and laughing mad they rolled their helmets round the lawn.
Lights came on across the city.

Then the reporter from the Times arrived
and asked about controlling it
i.e. not laughing excessively at it.
'It's mind over matter,' I said.
But as soon as the joke opened its mouth,
he wet himself.
This was not reported in the Times.

Then, the joke leaked out
and folk everywhere were doubled up.
Women gave birth
and a pill was prescribed
to stop the laughter the morning after a night of mirth
and Health and Safety proofed the shed ten decibels thick.
As for the joke,
whenever I walk him on the Ings,
he always wears a muzzle.

I am a circle fancier
and keep one in the shed.
I don't know how it folds its wings
I've never seen its head.
I feel sometimes it stares at me
with a circle-centred eye
but I've never seen it laugh
I've never seen it cry,
and I've never seen a circle
with needs of any kind.
They simply sit in silence
self-contained and well-defined
reflecting on existence
what makes them what they are
the formulae that give them life:
πr^2 and $2\pi r$.

My Bottom

Winner of the Turner Prize.
Category - Living Art,
soft sculpture.

The critics acclaim it: aesthetic,
symmetry of cheeks.
The Guardian writes:

'never frowns, wrinkles,
does not blush' and then a long digression on what it thinks.

The Sun, succinct,
a picture on page 3,
The Art of the Bum,

and my bottom's on T-shirts, bags and mugs.
In glossy mags the designer bottom,
and The Times, transcendental, with feeling writes:

child of the full moon - white.

States of Mind

According to my mood I do different birds,
for example, if I'm depressed
I pretend to be a curlew
and make a sad and haunting call.
Manic, I do the tern,
plummet and squawk.
And, acrobatic, arms outstretched
I do the swallow over the lawn.
For mystery, sometimes, the oystercatcher on the edge of tides,
calling in darkness.
Thoughtful, I stand on one leg,
alert and watching.
Opportunist, I do the starling
and scissor open plastic bags
and like the rook, sometimes I walk and sometimes hop
and when I feel life has no meaning
raucous across the fields I shout:
farce, farce, farce.
Unnoticed I do the humble sparrow
and when I feel I must escape
I arch the oceans with the swift.
Like many folk with no singing voice
I imagine myself an opera star
and do the blackbird on the garden fence.
Kestrel-like I keep an eye on things.
For silence glide with the tawny owl,
the golden oriole a splash of sun.
For courting, I do the crested grebe
shake my head and preen and dive.
I do this in a square down town
and make the ladies gifts of weeds,
and like a crane
breeding mad, jump up and down.

Hands

I look at these twins:
each four freckled fingers
and bossy thumbs -
moons half-rising in the pink of nails.

I look at these twins -
the dominant sibling grasping the pen,
the left more shy,
but holding the page as a brother might.

I look at these hands as ancestral hands
gathering stones on a shaggy moor,
struggling to build in the gaunt wind's rage
as a man who makes poems lifts words into place.

I look at these hands that glow against light
and know in this blood -
the blood of my son, the son of his son,
what seemed to be distant
grows warm in my palms.

Album

You a little girl patting your dog
long before we met
and me in black and white fishing on the Ings.
Your first camel and me acting daft.
Later you took my arm under the stars
and this is us on the beach.
The night warm. The sea muttering.
And here you were still asleep. Owls.
And that's us in the heather
you romping ahead frightening the grouse.
My seventieth birthday in the candlelight.
You moustached, wearing my cap.

For Banjo

If you love your dog, there's a good chance you'll love everything.

In the morning he came in,
ear split in a fight
and I put my arm round him, smoothed ointment on the wound.

Then we walked round the garden
and I was overcome by the enthusiasm of birds,
the otherness of woodlice,

not thinking much about much at all
only where I stood in the morning air
- the smell of roses and their redness,
irises.

I stroked his head and traced the flutings on bark
and felt a strange wonder for maggots on something or other.
I was drawn to the buddleia like butterflies,

moss on the wall.
Wind turned the leaves olive green to white
and I wondered what aphids thought, if they thought at all.

That night, her ear sore from an earring,
I soothed it with ointment.
My dog watched, head on one side.

There were murmurs down the lane.
Women in headscarves stood in groups.
In the pub it had gone beyond curious whisperings.
Grimaces.
Folk smouldering.
The relations gathered like clans, wild in hate.
First, they smashed his bicycle wheels,
then paint through the letter box.
I sat up in bed at night, praying it would stop.
All year forays of loathing.
His wife and dog paid the price
as if everything belonging to him was tainted.
Like me there were others: on the bus going to school,
in the Clifton on a Saturday night.
Tom Smith's father put a brick through his window.
I sometimes met him on the street with his wife,
my heart thumping I said "hello."
Her smile.
I never said anything to my parents.
A dark embarrassment,
and the hatred spread: the corner shop, the doctor's waiting room.
It was like smoking them out.
When I was twelve they went to Australia.
I often wondered about them and what they would do.
About her.

Starlings (For Emily and Ben)

The starlings were dying. We didn't know why.
We found two beneath the laurel - freshly dead,
the sheen of life on their feathers still.
We put them in shoe boxes.

On the wireless everyday George V,
lying in state. Soldiers by his catafalque.
Long glum queues. We wondered what he looked like dead,
wearing his pyjamas.

The starlings. It was their silence surprised us most.
All the din in the hawthorn tree,
singing with wings partly open.
Once they mobbed a crow. On the lawn stabbed.

We thought of George V jolted round London in his gun carriage.
All day my parents listened to the wireless. Dead music,
and the newspaper came - sheets of it. Black.
His life in the navy.

At Windsor he was buried in the vaults.
He'd last longer there, we thought.
We'd learnt about the Pharoahs and mummification,
lead and gold coffins.

For burial we wrapped the starlings in flags the size of handkerchiefs,
then thought that a waste of flags
and lay them straight into the grave we'd dug
- glints of blue, green, red in the afternoon sun.

We made mimic bugles with our hands and played the last post.

It was the day after the blitz:
early morning and a redness hung over the city,
smoke in stillness. No school.
Pickering Terrace no longer there,
and in Baker St. an unexploded bomb.
On both sides of the railway, houses smouldering.
The Germans had followed the silver lines in moonlight.
Everywhere police, troops. Keep out.

That Spring we jogged to the Ings,
shirts tied round our waists.
Pale bodies. Ribs.
Every holiday we came to see what we could see:
skylarks' nests - in hollows in the ground hidden by grass-
meadow pippits , swallows swerving above your head
and once we saw a fox. We followed it.
And always midges, insects - clouds of them
each alighting on its own kind of grass.
It was a warm Spring and we loved to jungle on the Ings.

Then between the Yorkshire Mist and the rusty sorrel
holes like we'd never seen before - five of them -
and we peered down one of them
and in the slant of sunlight we could make something out
and Storky Jones slipped his long white arm down
and pulled it up with a sucking noise, coated in mud,
and us on all fours staring at it,
like the moment you land a prize fish.
And then Storky Jones fetched up another
and soon we had five
and we ran down to the river and washed them
and there were numbers and letters on them.
We clutched our trophies to our chests.
Storky Jones - white as the warm Spring clouds
clutching a khaki bomb to his chest.
We kept them in a shed.

Chocolate Cake, Fishing and the Germans

I was in the lane studying the cobbles when my Mother turned the corner
- felt hat, legs that seemed to be shedding her stockings –
and she did what she usually did:
light up her fag and talk to me in the yard about what was right:
never telling lies, using folk and always being straight.
Then my Father jumped off his bike
took his clips off and lit up a Woodbine.
You could tell what day it was by the stubble on his chin.
Then we all had a cup of tea and a piece of chocolate cake.
'That was the bestest piece of chocolate cake I've ever tasted in my life,' I said.
My Father growled about the Hun
and quoted Churchill about fighting on the beaches,
but I was munching my Mother's chocolate cake
and thinking about fishing. I loved fishing and so did my Dad.
He thought it was British, like cricket.
'Do you think the perch will be rising tonight beneath the willows?' I asked.
After tea we had another piece of chocolate cake.
'Absolutely yummy,' I said
and felt the chocolate stuck deliciously to the roof of my mouth.
Then we all went down to the Ings
and my Father took his greenheart rod and me a rod he'd made out of willow
and my Mother took a large wedge of chocolate cake,
overhead Halifaxes throbbing.
'I bet the Hun knows nowt about fishing, nor chocolate cake,' I said.
There were midges over the water and you could see the fish were rising,
and I asked my Father if my line needed waxing.
Then we all had another piece of chocolate cake
and my teeth sank into its ice-thin coating of chocolate deep into the softness.

'Upstream,' I said, 'upstream. Let's go upstream.'
Downstream was through the city - quays, houses.
Upstream: whatever was in the reeds, round the next bend.
So early morning we rowed upstream, my father and I,
along the familiar banks we'd walked upon,
but from the river this was another country
- the willows touched the water, rising, falling,
dripping silver in the morning light.
A waterhen, head bobbing, paddled furiously into the reeds.
We dipped our oars and floated
and a lone grebe dived.
We wondered how it had got so far upstream.
A breeze riffled the water scattering the light of the weak sun
and a large fish jumped.
Even as it broke the surface 'Pike,' my Father said,
and he whispered about whatever it was he glimpsed in the reeds,
deep in the water.
Swallows swooped low, for this was the season of many insects
and we made for a little beach, two wagtails flicking the sand.
Then we took out our rods and mass of heaving maggots
and fished for roach rising a few feet from the bank.
Late afternoon a mist came down
and out of the mist wings slamming the air
and a pair of swans touched down upstream
- whiteness on the darkening waters.
My Father said nothing.

I was four or five
and terrified of his cap,
the soft humiliation of it
and his boots, coal black, standing beside me,
fearing to hate him lest he'd find out.

Under the tap he held my head,
execution by water
and once he lit with twist my acorn pipe.
I reeled and vomited down the lane
- a cure for smoking, aged six.

The Cockerel - Rhode Island Red -
harried the hens and leapt on my back.
He grabbed its neck and stretched it out.
It twitched on the ground,
my bowels in turmoil.

Midsummer 1936, I was seven then,
pneumonia struck.
I dare hardly think of the great release
- wickedness, sin.
And God might punish me by making him better.
I glanced at his eyes, half-shut, watery
as if the cold blue ice was melting then.
He gripped my hand with the strength he lifted ladders high,
sacks of corn.
He gripped and gripped.

For my Mother

Sometimes I do the pools
and feel my Mother's guiding hand,
quiet pressure of faith
- Arsenal 1, Liverpool 2 ...

On Saturday nights when results were read,
her studious reverence awed us kids
as she checked her coupon again and again
and again on the Sabbath in the News of the World
- York City 1, Grimsby 2 ...

Except for 3/6 when all teams drew
she never won,
yet her faith survived each week's results,
each season's:
York City 5, Liverpool 1.

Heron

In the half-light I thought it was a branch of the old conifer.
His blue-slate back glinted in the sun.
He was not here for water, fish.
This was a place to rest.
I wondered where he'd come from in the dark
and where he was going
head held high, black cap, wisps of feathers.

(As a child I mimicked his walk, slow motion of legs and shot out my arm
like a heron's long neck, my hand a beak.
I hid in the reeds till darkness came down,
the curious mists.)

From my conifer the heron flew off
flapping ponderously over hedgerows, fields
and I wondered where he'd fish that night,
in what strange waters, legs like reeds.

On Going Back

The waiter takes out of his pocket a cardboard mask and puts it on.
It smiles graciously.
He leads us to the table painted on the wall.
The wall is derelict.
He paints two chairs and sits us down.
The food - cut out of paper.
Your laugh - pages of the Press in the quickening wind.
He cuts a cup of coffee out.
Round our feet a paper bag
rubs itself.
On the fetid wall a cockroach
antennae weighing up.
You light a match.
My paper fingers tremble.

It was the light that kept me
- medieval windows, reds, blues.
Outside the red military. It was someday or other,
but it was the old dog, running aimlessly
- it was the dog that kept me,
or the crows on the chimney stacks.
It may have been the crows that kept me.
In a window, a mannequin.
Nothing else. It was the emptiness that kept me.
Wires in the wind's drift.
Rooftops slicing the sky.
The river - a wrapper bobbing.
The horse droppings - burnt sienna
and geese flying to infinity.
They kept me.
On the privet, light on the spider's web.
That's what kept me.

Second Thoughts

Overnight I've grown an extra finger on each hand,
looking down twelve toes.
I dare not face the mirror
there's something about my nose.
Twice as well I hear all sound
twice as well I see.
If I didn't have a double brain,
I'd doubt my sanity.

Horse

His withers rippled.
His mane no one ever combed,
bedraggled in the wind.
Ginger-roan, he lifted his tail
his droppings not far from the colour of his coat.
From the cart I looked behind to see how they'd fallen
and watched the steam.
Beneath the straps, his back rubbed bare.
An old horse when first I met him.
Blood shot eyes. Bellows of breath.
He rarely neighed. Snorted up hill.

Evening and I led him to the field.
He nuzzled my hand. His breath down my neck.
He rolled on his back. I lay beside him.
He stood like a king in his own greenness
and if he neighed that day, this was when he neighed
- over the hedges, fields. Then like a colt he bounded away.
I ran after him shouting his name.
The crows came home.
The sun down the long hillside.
I often wondered what he did all night, in darkness.

My Pet Hate

I keep my pet hate in the garden shed
and watch it through the window.

I jump up and down and swear at it,
make faces at it.
It cowers in the corners of the shed.

Sometimes I let it out on the garden lawn
and to make it move I poke it with a stick
and bawl at it, words like bugger and bastard.

Over the hedge, neighbours squint beneath their caps.
I hound it down the street and round the block.

Once it ran off. I missed the swine.
It came back.
I cursed it - sod and prat
and a host of words not fitting for a poem.
I glowered at it, jumped on it,
gobbed on it and kicked its backside.
It liked that.
My pet hate thrives on hate.

Manic Depression

I keep my manic depression in the garden shed.
You never know what mood he's in.
Sometimes in darkness he lingers for days,
so you grab him by the scruff of the neck and drag him out,
bawl at him, give him little tasks like cutting the grass,
but he slouches round the garden lawn
and so you try another tack:
hold a rose under his nose
or your head on one side at the recital in the hawthorn tree
- blackbird, thrush, but to no avail.
And then, one morning you open the door and he rushes out,
praises daisies, rolls in the grass
and from his head a thousand thoughts all fledging at once,
writes poems all night, paints,
and marvels how yesterday's tetchy birds sing today like nightingales.
And then the mists, and his mood dies back like greenness in Autumn
and dark winds whirl round the garden shed.

Before

(i)

He collected pebbles (which would never be so bright again) washed by the sea
and poked beneath the seaweed for the small crabs that hid there.
Together we stood in the undertow on little islands of sand
dissolving between our toes as the tide came in.
He stared out to sea
and whatever it was about distance, the ebb and flow,
you could see it in his eyes following the waves
- folding, collapsing,
spotting one that would break largest of all.

A cormorant stood on a rock drying its wings,
then dived, surfacing yards away.
'How long can it hold its breath?' he asked
and 'How do fish breathe?'

I took him down to the harbour, gulls in broken circles raucous
and we watched the fishing boats unloading into the fish market
- haddock, whiting, cod -
silver scales stuck to barrels, boxes.
'But their eyes are still open,' he said
and stared into the yellowish iris of a cod, the large dark pupil.
We walked across the corrugated sands. Lugworm castings.
The seaweed flowing in the undercurrent.
In the water a shadow and we waited till the sun went down for whatever it was.

On the southern side of the Taurus - an ancient rumour:
something immense, dark, prowled in the foothills.
There were those who glimpsed it in the mist, the forest's green darkness,
in the corn.
All Summer long we followed rumours of it like tracks from village to village
- footprints baked hard in the Summer sun,
and once an ancient headless carcass.

Late at night (lanterns swinging in the moonless dark)
the fire of eyes - lone wolf, fox -
and sometimes in the long grass a bending of stalks,
and from the wood darkness stirring.

Hattusha

To introduce her to Hittite History I took her to Hattusha
and we stopped at the Lion's Gate.
Two monoliths, two lions roaring out of stone,
and she talked to them, stroked them
and I told her how the Hittites dressed
- conical hats with flaps, kilts
and she touched an ant with a blade of grass
and like a child balanced on walls,
surprising lizards in the drowsy heat.
She pushed an iris almost up my nose
and traced the lichens on Hittite gods:
Tehup and Hepatu,
between them moss.
She stroked the moss. A swallow flew low.

For Ainslee

Her friends:
Joyce fetching tit bits to tempt her taste buds,
Maureen irises
and someone brought a book she never read.
Pure water her sustenance
and every night I lit the lanterns
- Amisus, the Taurus.
Shadows. Soft moths,
and once in half-sleep I heard her whisper
nightingales, the Bosphorus.
One morning she asked me to read her will again, aloud,
uneasy about equations of love and figures.
'And what do you think' she asked, 'have I been fair?'
I re-arranged the flowers.

And there were years with not much left to say
but now all the old imagery on the incoming tides
- Bythnia to Termossos, Aspendos.
Along the Dee – oystercatchers, guillemots
and from her window clematis, her bed of herbs.
'Tomorrow Cookeridge,' she said,
'Take a day off and go to York, I'll be back by night.'
Her lovely deceit.
I placed each item in her small case.
Her gown - diaphanous.
Kisses and frail goodbyes.
'Tomorrow love,' she said, 'tomorrow night.'

Everyday we went down to the beach
spray, gulls
and Hilbre Island in the running tides.
On the mudflats guillemots. Oystercatchers
and we walked the miles towards them
cold freshness on our faces
and sometimes at night in half-sleep we'd hear them
on the edge of tides
calling, calling,
and she'd talk of what we'd do in Spring
- Chester to Hoylake along the rocks
and beyond, to where the estuary meets
the darkening waters.

Geranium

You have glowed all summer long,
spluttered in rain, stood sturdy in wind
and I am vociferous about your colour
- touch you, talk to you.

Folk think I'm mad,
but you're only here for a few short months,
so I tend you all summer:
snip off dead flower heads, velutinous leaves
mimicking sometimes petal-red,
drench you in the arid sun.
If I were a painter, I'd love to paint geranium red.

We could go to the moors
and I'd show you fireweed and sunsets,
but all that you know,
and in Autumn in the bedraggled wind your last few petals cling
glowing still.

I see them in the dark,
the first frost.

In the Shed

A pair of old shoes
bear the imprints of wearing
- the mound of a toe
and the foot's slight side bulge,
sanctuaries in winter for sheltering mice.

An old felt hat
- a hive last summer for chanting bees
now a ruin for winds,

and an arthritic glove,
holed at the tips by fingers at evening locking the shed
- a mooring this year
for a chrysalis.

Poem for Christmas

The traffic has been annoying me all 1998
so I got up early this morning and rolled up all the roads.
I presented one-way signs to inflexible councillors
'No Left Turns' and 'No Right Turns'
to politicians of appropriate parties
and No U turns to Lady you know who,
cats'eyes to cats' homes
and large P's for Parking to public urinals;
zebras and pelicans are back in zoos
and childless couples have received school patrols,
schools - lollipops;
and to celebrate Christmas, New Year
traffic lights have been despatched to outer space for the festive touch
and the poet in everyone of us is afoot everywhere
hooting in the fumeless air.

there was a woman
who floated her husband on a piece of string
and drew him in to wash the car and dig the garden
and then she floated him up again
so most of his time was spent up there
with men and women on pieces of string
floating together behind the clouds
but what their spouses didn't know down below
was life up there was a sort of lark
a kind of spree fandango balero
a jamboree of floating bodies
festive free
rolling on air
and when their spouses drew them down
they always said it's tough up there

They've planted plastic roses,
imported a neon moon,
invented a bird that composes
a computerized change of tune;
for regularized emotions
it cries, it laughs, it sings;
they've glued it to a cypress
and made it flap its wings,
and lest all should go unnoticed,
to marvel at these things,
they've imported concrete lovers
to stare at the neon moon,
to listen eternally speechless
to a computerized bird with a tune.

Early morning and I sit at the window, coffee in my hand,
and wait for the trees to step out of the mists.

The starlings chatter
and the grasses have given up the summer struggle.
A hover-fly inspects the toadflax.

This is the time of day I like best
- a leaf spinning on the dog rose,
the last snow of the Russian vine
and on the shed the architecture of the passion flower.

The Daddy Long Legs has come inside.
A heron stands at the garden's end,
going nowhere.

I am a keeper of the letter z's
- zygote, zwiebank, zanella,
zebra of course,
zoo and its offspring:
zoolite, zoophyte, zoogonidium
- a linguistic safari for dictionary-bibbers,
origin hunters.

Some you'll recognise straight away
- zeal and zest from the same litter.
Some graze in flocks
maze and daze
and recent strains
-American stocks - burglarize, collectivize.

And in the long summer grass
some you hear but never see
erase and says,
enthusiasm and its throaty growl.
They leech to the 'Os
- knows and snows.

And the zigs and the zags bound this way and that,
zingiberaceous lurks in the shadows.
The zetas and zayins run in packs.

Once upon a time there was a number
who gave both sons equal sums to multiply
and asked for accounts x years on.
The first increased his sum by the power 'n'
and the number his father was squared with pride.
The second could add and subtract
but lacked the ability to multiply
and his sum remained constant,
so his father, the number, added the second son's sum
to the first son's sum
who multiplied and multiplied,
as, of course, did the Father's pride
his faith confirmed in multiplicity,
unconfused by relative ability.

Starling

There is this starling that lives in my head
and mocks other birds.
You'd swear my head was full of birds,
finches and blackbirds
linnets and things.

Of course, there are cuckoos
turkeys, hens and crows,
and I soar round the garden,
arms outstretched.

But it's not all chatter, song and squawk,
- in fashion, for instance
I wear greens and blues
iridescence for Sunday best,
glimpses of red and gold sometimes,
and it's not all poetry,
raucous I jostle
waddle and stab.

Before

(ii)

Before it was all peeping under stones
- black scorpions dazed by light,
grass snakes,
crossing Anatolia in green rain.
One night he brought a jar of fire flies to light our room
and on the plateau with a blade of grass fished for spiders,
wolf-spiders that lived in holes in the ground.
We lay on our backs,
stars shooting out of blackness,
and on the Black Sea, black storks
wading in the Spring rain.
Once he woke me to listen to the nightingales
and out of the black earth fetched an earring from the Acropolis
- gold. Then crosses and oil lamps and we climbed Termossos
and tiger moths glowed,
and by the wood we stopped and listened

- Scops owl
jackal,
wolf howl.

Sheer silence climbed the mountains.

Us Fingers

Together we shave, play the piano,
tickle, paint.
Singular, poke and pick,
furious sometimes make a fist,
nervous shake.
One of us injured, none of us grasps.

Our tips detect the next step upwards above the shale
or tremulous touch a violin, a hand perhaps.
A theatre of shadows on the wall,
all of us dreamers in the dark
- a half moon rising in every nail.

That day by the sea
- the day we fished and crabbed in pools
seaweed trailing in the undercurrent
and the tide going out,
and whatever it was it left behind
I put in my rucksack
pebbles - reds and blues.
I stared in the pools at their sheen of colour.
Driftwood, shells
and from the rocks ammonites
and my Mother waving
and shouting something over the waves
and the sea replying in many voices.

Spray over the path
and both of us drenched.

Balding

At the receding of the temples
- the first symptom of blight -
I scoured Boots and Timothy Whites
and the dubious columns of Playboy, Men Only
for the ultimate potion
arresting, reversing
the lessening of hair,

but nothing worked,
and so I clung to the remnants
- a few strands for damage limitation
across the shy baldness of my head.
Intensive care
- a gentle combing, coaxing
Tesco's Virgin Olive Oil
and someone suggested garden manure.
Desperate, I eyed it.

Nearly all gone
I like to think it's there somewhere under the skin.
There're symptoms of it
down your nose,
from your ears a sprig.

My head is now a Pharaoh's famine,
utter defoliation like the Russian steppes
compounded next with snowy age
- a wintry background
against the dome of the Corn Exchange -
and my wife, bless her, used to say
'bald and silver, you look distinguished.'
Bald and baldness, the very words shivered my innards
and 'distinguished' the end of life as I knew it then,

but the mind adjusts to anything
and what was pivotal as a young man
faded into history long ago.
Who remembers last year's snow
last year's leaves
or my bald embarrassment viewed from behind.

Anyway, what's left I've had it all shaved off - No 1
- the ultimate camouflage,
so no one knows if I'm bald or not,
slaphead and happy I rave and rock.

disorientation

eyes
I roll and weigh them in my palms
hold up to light

angular abandoned
arms and legs
unanchored thighs

and like a row of dominoes collapsed
the spine

lungs like balloons
have drifted somewhere

my nose where my mouth was
is eating air

elbows for heels
I'm hinged
in new places

my head
like a football
bounces away

I shout after myself

Shoes

My two shoes, scuffed in the shed
one beached on its side
one still afloat.
Laces - ropes of rigging, greened.

I wore you like a belief
under the stars
- cobbles, ice.
Moorings in darkness,

and I'll write you a poem
on shaping my life
in shaping yourselves to the shape of my feet,
compose
a litany of meekness.

Before

(iii)

Partridges whirred and eagles easy on thermals brought us to Anatolia,
your eyes skittering in light.
The summer wolf shimmered
and fireflies danced across Asia.
Nightjar. Fox.

Scops owl silent on its underdown,
rhythm of crickets,
and all was sap and joy
and you ahead in early Anatolian light.

Then rain - unseasonal rain,
rain hiding the shooting stars
filling ravines up to their necks
and you setting out across your secret terrain
and I not knowing how to follow.